The

Old-timer

Talks

Back

Here's to you and yours with
warm Vermont Greetings!

Allen R. Foley

Dartmouth Bookstore
Hanover - N. H.
- 1975 -

Illustrated by John Devaney

More snappers, whoppers, japes

and drolleries, as—

The Old-timer

Talks

Back to Allen R. Foley

*Professor Emeritus
of American
History
Dartmouth College
and Celebrated
Author of*

What the Old-timer Said, etc.

The Stephen Greene Press

Brattleboro, Vermont

This book has been produced in the United States of America. It is published by The Stephen Greene Press, Brattleboro, Vermont 05301

ISBN 0–8289–0258–5
Library of Congress Catalog Card Number: 75–16578

75 76 77 78 79 9 8 7 6 5 4 3 2 1

Contents

What the Old-Timer Said

The above is the title for the sampling of quips and stories I've run into during a half-century of forays into Vermont back-country, and the little book seems to have yielded pleasure to more folks than I ever imagined would see it. It has brought funny, friendly, and I may say, enthusiastic responses not only from all over America, but also from England, France, Spain, and even Japan. Many of the letters were from Americans in residence there, some native Vermonters or with Vermont connections. These people are apparently glad to be reminded of a way of life that has somehow uniquely characterized our North Country.

You recall the old-timer's statement that just because the cat gave birth to her kittens in the oven doesn't mean that they're biscuits. Place of birth, I have the firm notion, doesn't absolutely brand us with an indelible mark.

If the truth must be known, I was born in Massachusetts, about a month before the signing of the treaty ending the Spanish-American War, and I was educated in the schools of Framingham and at Dartmouth College, just across the Connecticut River from Norwich, Vermont. I spent long summers during student days in Maine at Tenants Harbor, devoted a happy year to the study of history at the University of Wisconsin, one more as an instructor at Dartmouth, and three at Harvard. This was followed by a gloriously leisurely trip around the world which, through the kindness of friends, was at no cost to me. Why I was so lucky, I'll never know.

Returning from that trip I rejoined the Dartmouth faculty and some years later, in 1941, took up residence in Norwich. This was just a few months before the Pearl Harbor holocaust. I've been in Norwich ever since.

But I get ahead of my story. W. C. Fields used to say that when he was born folks came for miles around to take a look: they weren't sure just what the little thing was. Happily I was not quite in that class, but—unlikely though that may seem to people who know me today—I was a puny child and folks wondered how long I would survive.

It was because of this early sickliness that the Green Mountain State entered my life, because as boys my younger brother and I were sent for a number of summers—in that blessed period before World War I—to spend several weeks at the farm of Uncle Charlie and Aunt Mary in Newark. Charlie and Mary weren't really related to us, being old friends of my mother's family, and they certainly gave us as boys a wonderful taste of old-time country living.

I remember there were cows on that farm and what must have been a fairly gentle bull. There were pigs and horses, both for work and riding, and a hard-working dog, and the inevitable cats. The dog was hard-working because there were lots of sheep to keep in line, and there were two rams which, as I remember, operated the small treadmill that ran the machinery used in separating the milk and churning butter.

Strange things stand out in a long memory. We drove occasionally to Lyndonville, and one day Uncle Charlie took us to Vail Manor, now incorporated into Lyndon College but then the country place of Theodore N. Vail, at that time the president of American Tel & Tel. Although the family were not in residence we were shown through the house, and I remember the twin towers and a secret staircase and especially a throne-like seat over Mr. Vail's private toilet—he was a large man as I recall—with the inscription

HERE I TAKE SOLID COMFORT

For some reason I remember, too, an early buggy ride. The family were in two buggies, I in the second one with Aunt Mary, and as we were going toward Burke Hollow Uncle Charlie came running back toward us in high excitement, waving his arms. What had happened was that Charlie had met an automobile on the road, a Maxwell roadster I think, and was coming back to help us get by. Automobiles were that rare then. He got the buggy well over to the side of the road and held the horse's bridle firmly while the car chugged slowly by. Charlie was civil to the driver and thanked him for his help. But he let go when the car had disappeared in a cloud of dust.

"Damn 'em!" he said, or something to that effect. "They can have those contraptions in the city if they want to. But why in the devil do they invade God's country?"

It wasn't so many years after this that I was back, boning up on some Latin in the Clark School in Hanover and living with Sherm Somerville's family on their farm out on the turnpike in Norwich. It was good to be in Vermont again, and it was a pleasant summer with good progress toward an exam for Latin credits for admission to college. Sherm was quite a character, and I picked up a lot of expressions from him. One I find myself using every now and again: "Talk's cheap; but damn it, it takes money to buy rum!"

In the Fall of 1916 I entered Dartmouth as a freshman. Even undergraduates travelled in those distant days by train and disembarked at the old Norwich-Hanover station in Norwich. There was usually horse-drawn transportation across the Connecticut river bridge into Hanover, but most of us walked up West Wheelock Street to town—a climb more often than not referred to as "that goddam hill."

Happily, Vermont was not out-of-bounds, and we hiked through her back-country a lot in those days. Often on Saturday afternoons we'd walk down the railroad tracks on the Vermont side, stopping once in a while to play a game of duck-on-the-rock, or visiting at a well-established hobo camp. We'd get a meal at the old Junction House (now Hotel Coolidge), perhaps stir up a little hell in White Town, then walk back to Hanover on the New Hampshire side, sometimes singing vigorously.

I know that all this sounds simple-minded to the undergraduate of today. But as Charles Dana Gibson once said, reminiscing about his happy youth, "If I remember correctly, we had a pretty good time then too."

A few of us got acquainted with the station agent upriver at Pompanoosuc, the next train stop north of Norwich, and at times we headed that way. Harry, the agent, was then a bachelor, and his mother kept house for him in what had been the old station across the tracks from the new one. She would always say, "You boys must stay for supper" —and we always did. And though she might say she really didn't have much to offer we'd always sit down to a table of good victuals and plenty of them. Then we'd sit around and talk and listen to the old Edison phonograph.

Towards nine o'clock Harry would remind us that the way-freight would be coming down pretty soon. We'd go over to the dark little station, where Harry would get his lantern and flag the engineer down. We all piled into the cab, visited with the engine crew on the way south, and when the train slowed down for the Norwich station we'd hop off. It was probably a violation of the rules, but no one ever came to harm and we had fun.

Then there were the so-called "deputation trips" when three or four undergraduates went

out to spend a weekend in some small community. A visit to Bradford sticks in my mind. There were two co-operating churches across the street from each other, one Congregational and the other Methodist. Contrary to what you might expect, the Methodist preacher was a jolly fellow and the Congregationalist was a serious-minded sober man. At the Sunday evening service they planned to take up a collection to pay for our train fare, which was the only cash involved in the entire weekend. The meeting was held in the Congregational Church, but the Congregational minister said he would rather not be the one to ask for the collection since his Methodist brother had "a way about such things." The Methodist agreed to do it, but warned his Congregational brother that he would do it in his own fashion.

After stating what the purpose of the collection was, and how much the community had enjoyed having these Dartmouth boys here with us, he closed his appeal by saying, "My eyesight is not too good, but Brother Alexander has eyes like a hawk, especially when watching the collection plate, and God help the person who doesn't put in at least a quarter."

Well, as I said, I travelled around a bit after leaving college, learning a little history and something about teaching it. I recall three sticky summers in New York City where I taught at Columbia. Finally I was back in Dartmouth and World War II was upon us.

It was during the war, when I was going from St. Johnsbury to Swanton on the old St. J. & L.C. Railroad, that I found myself sitting in the baggage car next to O. W. M. Sprague, a professor at the Harvard Business School. We were in the baggage car, I remember, because the small passenger section was full, and they'd placed rocking chairs for us where we could look out the open car door and admire the wonderful sweep back to the White Mountains.

The Professor, I remember, knew a great deal about the building and financing of this railroad some seventy years earlier, and he told how the company used camp-meeting methods, with music and entertainment preceeding the pitch for support, to raise money from the towns along the proposed route. The Professor told me he had found a partial press account of the chief promoter's talk given in the big tent specially erected at Hardwick. It ran something like this:

> "Ladies and gentlemen of Hardwick, we appreciate your attendance today and I want to make one last appeal for your support. Remember that this part of the railroad line is to be part of a projected trans-continental line of communication. The first step is to connect Portland, Maine, with Ogdensburg, New York, on the St. Lawrence River. Then through the Great Lakes we will hook on to a trans-continental line through to the Pacific Ocean, and by ship be open to the trade of the Far East.
>
> "Think, my friends! The town of Hardwick will then be directly connected with the fabled lands of China and Japan. Keep in mind the thrill which will be yours as you look up from your haying some fine summer day and see the express train go by: You'll catch a whiff of the private tea-stock of Queen Victoria being rushed from the tea fields of China direct to Windsor Castle."

When I retired from Dartmouth in June of 1964, my neighbors in Norwich sent me to the House of Representatives in Montpelier to represent the town. Decorum in that House, I found, is pretty impressive, and that's as it should be. But there are a couple of incidents I will pass along to you.

One year we had a bill dealing with the inoculation of dogs against rabies. It was a simple bill, and with a favorable committee report it should have breezed through the House without delay. But there are always members who suddenly get the urge to talk, and there was a lady so moved on this occasion who was recognized by the Speaker.

She first expressed her conviction that there were too many dogs in Vermont, elaborating rather fully on her feeling. Her next point was that the wrong people had dogs; and, while some might agree with this position, it had nothing to do with the bill at hand. Her third point dealt with the fact that dogs either by instinct or training or both always did their business in the neighbor's yard. She said that when she came out of the house, unless she was very careful, she'd put her foot in it. And when she tried to cut her lawn with a power-mower she got an unwelcome shower-bath.

The trouble with this kind of talk is that it invariably lures others to their feet. The member

from Poultney took the floor when the lady was through and inquired if something was wrong with the previous speaker. Didn't she know what a dog could mean in the life of a boy? "And," he added, "I want to tell the members of this House that a well-trained dog will behave in the house as well, if not better, than a well-trained child." The member from Craftsbury then took the floor to make a sharp rebuttal: "The trouble with the last speaker, Mr. Speaker, is that perhaps he doesn't realize that to train a dog you've got to know more than the dog does."

Then a usually dignified member from Montpelier put his oar in. "Mr. Speaker, I have a solution to at least one of the lady member's worries. That is, to put britches on the bitches." And so it continued until a member from Brattleboro suggested we call it quits, with an entry in the House Journal that this was the day when "the House went to the dogs."

The House of 1973 included an unusually large percentage of young members. A member from Bennington, aged 25, was responsible not only for an excellent move but one that also brought a lively laugh from the members. It concerned a somewhat foolish resolution designed to make Vermont's Dairy Queen the State Hostess of the year.

Resolutions, it should be explained parenthetically, may be offered by any member, and, without consultation or consideration by committee, may be put to immediate vote of the House. Or, by motion, a resolution may be treated as a bill and referred to an appropriate committee for consideration; without such consideration, however, the House is likely to vote favorably on resolutions, be they good, bad or indifferent.

The young member from Bennington rose and spoke as follows:

"Mr. Speaker, I am opposed to this resolution and opposed in principle to such beauty contests in general. They degrade womanhood. You put nice girls on parade before a big crowd—sometimes a leering crowd—and judge their appearance in an unseemly fashion. It's like a cattle show. I therefore move, Mr. Speaker, that this resolution be treated as a bill and referred to the Committee on Agriculture."

By a loud affirmative voice vote of the House, it was so referred, and there, happily, it died.

Another story has to do with State symbols. Vermont has some fine ones—the sugar maple is the state tree and the Morgan horse the state animal, etc. The trouble seemed to be that Vermont does not have a state rock. A lady member proposed a bill which would give that honor to a rock called green schist. Now green schist is plentiful in Vermont. It can be frequently seen along road-cuts on the new interstate throughways, where it takes on a lovely soft green color when wet.

Probably the only drawback to adopting green schist as the state stone is that its name must always be pronounced, to avoid misunderstanding, with great care and clarity.

The wags were soon on their feet. One member observed that it was a good choice because there was so much of it in Vermont. Another favored the suggestion because it was so easily picked up along the roadside. A third questioned the choice because Vermont would then have to be known as the Green Schist State. After more of the same, the matter was referred back to the committee for further study. If memory serves, we never heard about the matter again.

The Judiciary Committee of the House had under consideration a bill the purpose of which was to reduce what was viewed by some as large-scale and objectionable nudity in certain areas of the state, including what is known as skinny-dipping. At lunch one day I asked a member of that committee what the committee was going to do with that bill. He replied in a semi-confidential tone, "I doubt if that even sees the light of day." Whereupon a long-time member who was sitting with us commented, "Well now, it's all right after dark anyway."

The Vermont Senate is a notably dignified body —most of the time. But I recall one Windsor County senator who spoke in favor of a bill to allow farmers living in the back-country to place small signs on the main roads to advertise their produce to the traveller. He pointed out how helpful and even essential such signs were, both for seller and buyer. And especially, he said, in the case of remote farms almost impossible for the stranger to locate. He knew of one such farm in Windsor County, the senator observed, so remote that they had to keep their own tom cat.

Well, tom cats are way off the subject. What I started to say was that my earlier book, WHAT THE OLD-TIMER SAID, seems to have amused and pleased quite a few people. In view of this unexpected response I have tried to collect here a few more little stories in the modest hope that these, too, may give pleasure.

Contrary Country

Very often there's sound advice in an old-timer's response to no matter how routine a question.

A friend of mine asked an old fellow, "How are you today?"

"God," was the reply, "I think I'm pretty good—unless you want to go into de-tails."

Last mud season my friend Will Atwood, driving me into Montpelier from Adamant, was reminded of the following story. I'm afraid I can't vouch for its truth.

Silas Smith, hopping across the flat in mud-time, spied Heber Brown's hat. So Silas reached out with a pitchfork and very, very carefully lifted the hat: and there was Heber, up to his ears in mud.

"Heber," observed Silas, "you're really in it."

"I'm OK," Heber replied. "But the team's in pretty deep."

There was no doubt about it that it was Heber Brown's son, Alfred, who got Ira's daughter into a peck of trouble. The fact is she was in a family way. So Ira went to talk to Heber about it.

As it happened, Heber wasn't there so Ira spoke to the hired girl instead. She tried to be helpful.

"I know Heber gets twenty-five dollars for the bull," she explained. "I don't know what he gets for Alfred."

An old-timer surprised me the other day with this:

"A bunch of us boys was sitting round the stove in Sam's store the other night, the way we have for years, talking about our neighbors and half-joking sometimes about each other.

"So I up and said: 'Do you know what we ought to call these sittin's? Well, if it was in the city, they'd be called group therapy sessions, and we'd be paying twenty-five dollars an hour for the treatment."

An out-of-state visitor with gourmet tastes stopped at a little restaurant in the northern part of the state. The elderly female proprietor came tottering in to ask what he wanted.

"Do you have frogs' legs?" the customer asked.

"Nope," replied the old lady. "I guess it's just my arthuritis."

Direction jokes are part of the landscape in our part of the world. Joel Carew at Dartmouth College used to tell this one, one of the best I think. To spare feelings, I've changed the name of the town.

A motorist came to a fork in a Vermont road. As usual, there was no sign to guide him.

"Which way to South Tinbrook?" he asked the aged countryman who was sitting on a nearby front porch. The man pointed toward the south road.

"Is it far?" the visitor asked.

"No, but when you get there you might wish it was a sight further."

A friend told me the other day about an experience he had driving back up into the hills of Windsor County on a windy winter's day. The dirt road not only led sharply uphill, but it curved and was desperately narrow.

Finally my friend reached the farmhouse and settled down in the kitchen to visit with the old fellow who lived there alone, a dog curled up at his feet and a cat purring by the stove. The visitor remarked about the steep and narrow road, and said it might be pretty bad if you met anyone coming the other way.

"Nonsense," replied the old gentleman; "nothing bad about meeting somebody on the road. It's the passing that's makes the trouble."

An old-timer named Wallace Gilpin, long since departed this world, used to publish a weekly paper called the *Orleans County Monitor*. It was a small-size, four-page sheet with an annual subscription price of one dollar. Wallace did just about all the work himself—gathered the news and ads, set the type, and ran it off on his little press.

The neighbors tended to be slow in paying up their subscription bills and every once in a while Wallace would go out collecting. One day he arrived in his Model T at a farm whose owner owed him for three years' back subscription. Their conversation went something like this:

> Wallace: "Well, Joel, I thought I'd see if I could collect some of the subscription money you owe me."
>
> Joel: "I'm sorry, Wallace, but I ain't got a damn cent."
>
> Wallace: "Couldn't spare me a dollar, Joel?"
>
> Joel: "Nope; I told you I ain't got a cent."
>
> Wallace: "Well, how about a nice little pig?"
>
> Joel: "Ain't got a pig on the place."
>
> Wallace: "What about a roasting chicken?"
>
> Joel: "Nope, no roasting chickens."

Wallace, disgusted, made one last try.

> Wallace: "Now, Joel, you wouldn't have a bag of nice clean corncobs, would you?"
>
> Joel: "Nope, I ain't got no corncobs. Why in hell do you think I keep subscribing to your paper?"

A small church in Addison County had gotten rather shabby, badly in need of painting and general refurbishing. The congregation decided to purchase the necessary materials and enlist contributions and volunteer labor from the village.

It all worked out well: the building was painted inside and out, the floors were sanded and polished, the pews were refinished, some of the electric fixtures were replaced. Even the lawn was improved.

Later the congregation arranged a get-together to express appreciation to all who had helped. The chairman of the Improvement Committee singled out major contributors and special workers, and paid tribute to each and all. When he appeared to have reached the end of his list a little old lady rose and spoke as follows:

"This is all very good and we do appreciate these improvements. But nothing has been said about the manure we put on the lawn. I want you to know that came through me."

The late June flood of 1973—the worst in Vermont in some forty years—fouled some of the local water supplies. In Norwich, for example, we were advised not to drink the town water for a while unless we boiled it first.

A friend of mine, some days later, called the Town Clerk to ask if it was safe now to drink town water. The response, in genuine old-timer style, was only:

"Nope. They're still biling."

Caleb was inclined at times, like some others we know, to take too much to drink. His wife, Mary, labored with him patiently and at long last, after about thirty years, he seemed to have gone over pretty well to the side of abstinence.

Then one night after an encounter with some cronies, Caleb came home no longer sober. Mary, disappointed and angry, finally said, "You're not to sleep in this house tonight, Caleb Jones. Grab yourself a blanket and go out to the barn." He went.

Along about three in the morning Mary roused from her sleep, reached over on her husband's side of the bed, and then suddenly remembered her rough treatment of Caleb. Remorseful that she had kept him out of his own house after thirty years together, she got up, lit the lantern, and went out to find him.

Mary expected to find him in the horse barn, but he wasn't there. She tried the cow barn: no Caleb. She couldn't believe he'd bed down with the pigs—but there she found him, sound asleep next to a friendly sow.

Presently he stirred in his sleep, turned toward the old sow and began running his hand along her belly. And as Mary waited in the corner she heard him mutter, "Mary, old gal, didn't remember you had so many buttons on front of your nightgown."

Weston Sayre, who used to live up the mountain back of Jericho, would came down to Burlington twice a year, and while there on one visit was side-swiped by the car of a tourist and knocked down. The visitor, frightened and solicitious, jumped from the vehicle and asked Sayre if he was hurt.

"Well," replied Weston, "it ain't done me much good."

This is an old, old story out of Orange County. A countryman was driving down to the village early one morning when he saw hanging from a limb of a tree near the road a fellow from a neighboring town who was not too well liked. On arriving in the village, the old-timer spied a friend and told him what he'd seen.

"God, Link," asked his friend, "didn't you cut him down?"

"Nope," was the level reply: "he was still a-twitchin'."

An old-timer who used to trap up in Essex County a good part of each year was asked if he'd ever been lost in the woods.

"Not lost, no. But I was awful bewildered for two days once."

Here's a story told by Admiral William S. Sims. It was during World War I when Sims and a couple of friends were staying overnight at the old St. Johnsbury house. Those were the days when a Vermont breakfast was a major undertaking, and the waitress rattled off a long list of tempting dishes, then added, "You can have 'em all if you want."

Sims and one of his friends contented themselves with bacon and eggs. But the third man in the party said he'd have the whole list—except for the apple pie.

"Land o' goodness," said the waitress. "What's wrong with our apple pie?"

Sims, on a tour of duty later in England, would often tell the story there. More than once, he reported, someone from the British audience would came up to him afterwards and ask: "By the way, Admiral, what *was* wrong with that apple pie?"

And of course you all remember the Bennington horse trader that was approached by the dude.

"What do you want for that mare?" the young man asked.

"I'll take a hundred and a half for her," the trader said. "But she don't look so good."

They discussed the pros and cons of the animal and finally reached agreement. The new owner paid and went off with his purchase.

He was back again the next day, mad as hops.

"What's the matter with that horse?" he demanded to know. "She ran me right off the road."

"Been blind for a year," the Benningtonian admitted. "Told you she didn't look so good."

Habit of Thrift

Some fifty years ago a couple named Brougham lived in what the maps call West Norwich but which is known locally as Beaver Meadow. The old man liked to chew tobacco, and when he'd gotten the goodness out of a chew he'd roll up the cud neatly and put it on the back of the kitchen stove to dry out.

Well, the old lady—and this is a true story— liked to smoke an old clay pipe. She would take the dryest cud at the back of the row, loosten it up a bit in her hand, then pack it into her pipe. It smoked right well, she claimed.

Now, this is not only a perfect example of rock-ribbed thrift; it also warms the heart of this old teacher, who has always claimed that history, in its strange fashion, does repeat itself. For Mrs. Brougham was anticipating by half a century one of our pet projects today: recycling.

A retired professor who now has a year-round place near Lake Fairlee reports this story.

A New York City family bought an old farm near by and proposed to fix it up in first-class style. They had a deed for 150 acres of land and thought that first they'd have the land surveyed and the boundary lines located. They wanted an

A-1 survey that would stand up in any court, and in their ignorance they figured that no surveyor in a little rural State could be relied on. So they brought a high-powered team of three civil engineers up from New York, at a cost which you can imagine.

They got on well with the survey except for one corner which they could not seem to locate. Seeing an elderly farmer swinging a scythe in a nearby field, they told him their problem and asked if he could help. The old-timer allowed as how perhaps he could, particularly as they promised to pay if he could locate this one corner.

So he started off, walked about a tenth of a mile, got down in some scrub growth, poked around a bit and then called out, "Here's your corner." The engineers agreed it was the one they were looking for. They thanked him for his help and handed him a card with their New York address, suggesting that if he would send them his bill they would see he was paid. A week or so later he mailed them a bill for a hundred dollars.

They replied that they were glad to hear from him and, although they rather felt his charge was excessive, they would pay it if he sent them an itemized accounting.

In due course it came: "$25 for finding the corner, $75 for knowing where it was."

Mrs. Tolby, who lived for years in a small house directly on the river north of Hanover, had a woodlot and after the death of her husband, hired her wood cut by a neighbor. He'd half filled the woodshed by nightfall one cold November day, so she asked him in for a glass of whiskey.

The old-timer finished his drink before commenting: "There was no such thing when I was a young 'un."

"Whatever do you mean?" asked the widow. "No whiskey?"

"Plenty of whiskey," he answered. "Never in such a small glass."

I'm indebted to Ed Mead, writer and Hanover, New Hampshire, neighbor, for an ancient story, a true one as far as I know, about an old farmer who stopped at the Tilton ticket office, back when it was still called Sanbornton Bridge. This is New Hampshire, mind you.

"How much to Littleton?" he asked the ticket agent.

"Two dollars."

The farmer said nothing for a bit. "Well then, how much for a cow?"

"Three dollars."

"A pig?"

"One dollar."

"Book me as a pig," said the old-timer promptly.

We are all familiar with the innocent-seeming stickers that decorate the windows of unsold cars in dealer showrooms. They start out with a "basic price" for the car. But then there follows a number of built-in items, such as power steering, undercoating, bumper guards, etc., that alter the total price, usually out of all recognition. In this story, you will be happy to know, the tables are turned.

For by a strange fluke of fate a local car dealer one day appeared at Perley Moore's hill farm wanting to buy a cow. Farmer Moore showed the dealer to the barn and told him to pick out an animal. The dealer examined the herd keenly, made his choice, and asked the price.

"That's a one-hundred-dollar cow," Moore replied without hesitation.

"Very reasonable," said the city man. "I'll take her."

"That's the basic price," Moore added, getting out a stub of pencil. "There are one or two extras of course." He did some figuring on a piece of paper, handed it to the dealer. This is what he had written:

Basic cow	$100.00
Two-toned exterior	45.00
Extra stomach	75.00
Storage compartment and dispensing device	60.00
Four spigots @ $10 each	40.00
Genuine cowhide upholstery	75.00
Dual horns @ $7.50 each	15.00
Automatic fly-swatter	35.00
Total:	$445.00

Town History

A couple from New Jersey were telling about their first winter in Londonderry. It was late in the year when they closed the deal for the house, but they decided to make the best of it and spend their first winter without central heat. A friendly neighbor warned that the cellar walls were laid up roughly with many chinks, and advised banking the house.

My down-country friends said they were well enough off financially with a good mortgage. But their neighbor explained that he wasn't talking about money but about putting up a little fence around the cellar walls and filling up the space to block the drafts. You could use sawdust or leaves or hay for this purpose, he told them, but probably the best insulation was cow manure. So he helped put up a fence and they banked the house with manure.

Just before the first snow came, the couple were visited by a lady friend from New Jersey, and she naturally wanted to know what all that mess was around the edge of the building. They explained. The visitor said she was going to enjoy telling this story to friends back home. Just as she was leaving, she asked a final question.

"But how in the world did you get all those cows to back up around the house?"

Walter Needham, historian of Guilford and co-author of that wonderful time-capsule of a Vermont classic, *A Book of Country Things,* tells of the founding of the Retreat, Brattleboro's pioneering mental hospital, something like this:

Richard Whitney, a lawyer of Guilford, seemed to be talking a little peculiar—this was way back at the start of the last century—so the doctors held him under water a while, as had been done to the Salem witches, then revived him.

Whitney still talked funny, so they put him back under the water—for a little longer this time. Still no improvement in Whitney's ways. So they kept at it in the same progressive fashion until finally he wouldn't revive at all.

Mrs. Anna Marsh, who had observed all this and didn't like it, left some money to be used for the mentally afflicted in Windham County, and that, they say, is how the Retreat got its start.

"Whitney," Walter reports, "is buried over in Hinsdale, and doctors have been using hydrotherapy ever since—with somewhat happier results of late."

Herbert Haskell, who had farmed well his acres on the Dover-Wilmington road, in his later years would oblige a neighbor or a proper-seeming transplant by sharpening shears or setting saws. When Jenny Evans was three years old and extremely tiny even for this early age, her father, Bol Evans, took her with him to visit Haskell and ask the old gentleman if he'd sharpen some mower blades.

After the usual amount of fore-talk, and the business concluded, Evans introduced his daughter, who was standing shyly near by. Mr. Haskell studied the diminutive girl a moment, then commented:

"Y' almost didn't get your seed back."

As that loyal Vermonter, Sheldon Dimick, tells it, he was being shown over an old house that was up for sale. It was full of hundreds of empty beer and whiskey bottles. They were in every room, filled every closet.

The old lady showing Sheldon around commented on this. He asked her:

"Do you mean to say the man who lived here drank all that himself?"

"Oh yes," she said. "He was a bad man. But the drink finally caught up with him."

"How old was he when he died?"

"Ninety-three."

Some years ago a storekeeper in Danville had two new cast-iron stoves come in from the manufacturer, and remembering that a customer down in Peacham had ordered one, he put the stove on his old pung and drove down some seven or eight miles to deliver it. It was a below-zero winter day in the North Country and, as he said, "It was a damn long, cold ride."

When the dealer arrived he set the stove up and started a fire to show it was in good working order. Unfortunately the sudden heat was too much for the cold iron. The stove cracked and split.

Although the dealer should have known better, he at least was resourceful: he drove back to the store, started a fire in the second stove, put it on the pung and drove all the way back to Peacham with a boy riding along to keep it stoked.

The old-timer remarked, "By god, Jeb, the boy kept warm even if you didn't."

A newcomer to town, a college man and all that, bought quite a piece of land, and was planning a very ecological-minded lumber operation.

But the natives found him peculiar: they couldn't get over the fact he always seemed to wear overalls and farm boots, a flannel shirt and a tattered straw hat. Sometimes he even had a piece of hay in his mouth.

"I don't know as there's anything really wrong with him," Old Will said judiciously one day down at the store. "He dresses like that 'cause he wants to look just like what city folks think we look like."

Mrs. Neil Malone, daughter of the Vermont attorney and author, Thomas Reed Powell, has told me some good stories about her family. Some have appeared in *What the Old-timer Said.* Now I'd like to pass a couple more along to you.

One her father liked was of the stranger who stopped by at the County courthouse in a small town in the Green Mountains and asked to speak to the Clerk of Court. The janitor told him he was over at the barber shop.

"When will he return?" inquired the stranger.

After taking good aim at the spittoon, the janitor replied, "When he's finished there."

The stranger explained that he had important business and must see him, and received the stern reply:

"Mister, you don't seem to know much about how we do things in our part of the country. What be your name?"

"Charles Evans Hughes, Chief Justice of the Supreme Court."

On her father's twenty-first birthday, Mrs. Malone says, Grandpa gave him a beautiful gold pocket watch. His presentation speech, in full, was as follows:

"Son, we'd always planned to give you a watch when you reached the age of wisdom. We've decided it's better not to wait."

Streaking, at the time of this writing, has not enlivened the Vermont scene to the degree experienced in some other states. But there have been a few demonstrations, including this one:

In a small town an elderly couple, both around 70, appeared one warm day trudging down Main Street clad only in shoes and, in the case of the man of the house, hat and necktie.

"My god," said a friend upon meeting them, "are you two streaking?"

"Nope," said the wife, "too old to streak. We're snailing."

Speaking of rocks, one old-timer was working in his Wardsboro garden when what the late Frederic Van der Water has dubbed a permanent summer resident stopped by and commented:

"You got a lot of rocks in that garden, haven't you?"

"Most two rocks to every dirt," was the reply.

A philosopher countryman has declared:

"I like a rock or two in a garden. Gives me something to tap my hoe on."

Comeback

Time was when city folk tended to underrate the old-timer, holding that wit and wisdom and such things originate in the city. A friend in Colchester was telling me the other day about two down-country types that spied an old gentleman at that endless occupation of New England hill farmers, digging the rocks out of his field (what the forms from Washington call "obstruction removal.")

The two city men stopped to have a little fun with the farmer. "What are you doing?" one of them asked.

"Picking stone," the farmer replied, going on with his work.

"Where did they all come from?"

The farmer still didn't look at them. "Glacier brought 'em," he replied.

"Where'd the glacier go?"

The farmer slowly stood up, and took a long look at the city men.

"Back to get some more stones," he said.

A gentleman named Eddy was summering on Lake Willoughby up north in Orleans County. He went into the Town Clerk's office in Westmore to ask if he could get a fishing license.

The elderly clerk, busy writing at a table, didn't look up from his writing, but answered, "Yes, take a chair."

Some time elapsed while the clerk continued his writing and Mr. Eddy, somewhat impatient, stated his request again and added, "I happen to be President of Chatham College in Pittsburgh, Pennsylvania."

The clerk continued his writing, never looked up, and replied:

"Take two chairs then."

At a church supper in North Thetford one of the waiters was a 14-year-old boy, put to work early as many country boys still are. A lady summer visitor had finished the main course and was asked by the boy if she'd like some dessert. She said she might and inquired what they were offering for dessert.

"Pie," said the young man; "apple and mince."

"What do you recommend?" she asked.

Following good native practice and cautions, his reply was: "I don't."

A certain pretty tight-fisted farmer drove his hired hand pretty hard, and at such times as he was getting his hay crop down and dried and in the barn, along with milking and the other chores, the hired man worked pretty much from sun-up to sun-down.

One evening, after a long day's work, as he and the hired man were milking the large herd—by hand, of course—the farmer remarked, "You know, Seth, sitting here milking is kinda restful to me."

"Well, maybe," said Seth. "But I don't know but I'd ruther go to bed tired."

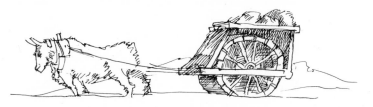

Then there was the old-timer who was getting deaf. His wife kept urging him to see a doctor: he'd know right away, she said, what could be done about it. The old man succeeded in putting his visit off for some time. But she kept after him and finally one day he found himself sitting in the doctor's office with the MD quizzing him closely:

"Jeb, do you smoke?"

"Hardly smoke at all."

"Drink?"

"Yes, well I drink a little," Jeb admitted reluctantly.

"You can't drink, you know: you've got to stop that." Pause.

"Don't think I'll do that."

The Doctor hitched his chair forward purposefully.

"Jeb," he said, "you're just going to have to quit drinking. If you don't, you'll grow stone deaf."

"Guess I'll get deaf, then," replied the old-fellow: "I like what I drink better'n what I hear."

In the first years of Mount Snow, before the ski resort had achieved much in the way of commercial lodgings, an old-timer and a friend were discussing the manners of strangers from down-country who virtually demanded to be put up, money no object and willing to rough it.

"What can you say to one of these birds," the friend complained, "when they bang on your door and ask how much you'd charge to let 'em sleep out in the barn with your bull?"

"I'd say ten dollars," the old-timer said: "*My bull's registered.*"

It was foliage season—early October, that is—and a tourist out cruising the back roads felt the need for immediate toilet facilities, so he stopped at a farm and knocked on the door. The lady of the house, learning of his need, directed the stranger to the privy out back. On arriving there, he discovered to his embarrassment that it was occupied by the farmer himself.

"No bother," said the farmer. "This is a two-holer. Come on in."

Later, as the farmer was leaving, a dime fell out of his pants and slipped down the hole. The farmer got out a large leather wallet, removed a five dollar bill, and tossed it down the hole.

"What in the world did you do that for?" the amazed visitor exclaimed.

"Mister," said the farmer, "you don't think, do you, I'd climb down in there for a dime?"

A prominent Cavendish lady was always mindful of those less fortunate in the community, and among other kind deeds always tried to invite some person outside the family, particularly someone who was alone and without relatives or friends, to share her family dinners on special days like Thanksgiving and Christmas.

One Christmas she decided to invite an eccentric handy man who could always be called on in time of need to do most anything, and who lived alone in rather squalid quarters. She met him on the street and extended her invitation. He thanked her, but said he'd have to think it over. One of his well-known peculiarities was that in the winter he would always wear several suits of long, heavy winter underwear, which he rarely changed, plus a couple of pairs of pants and several heavy shirts.

A few days later she met him again and he gave her his reply to the invitation:

"Now, Miss Gay, I thank you for your kindness, but I've been thinking it over and I just don't know. I'd have to take off all my clothes and take some kind of a bath, then try to find something else to wear. And, you know, Miss Gay, I've about decided that it ain't worth it."

A young Vermonter who had studied for the ministry became pastor of a church in a lively Green Mountain town. During student days he had taken up golf, and one of his parishioners, a city man who had retired to Vermont, used to invite him to play the game occasionally.

The city fellow, despite his years, was a better golfer than the young minister, and one day when they got back to the clubhouse the preacher was feeling despondent, for he had played a particularly poor game.

"Never mind, Reverend," said his friend, "you'll have the last word. You'll probably bury me."

"Maybe," said the young man. "But it will still be your hole."

Native courtesy is often remarked on by students of the back-country—even though, more often than not, it is relieved by straight-from-the-shoulder frankness.

An undergraduate friend of mine, a stranger to the area but anxious to get acquainted with the place, was wandering around one day in Windsor County. He stopped at a little village store and asked the old proprietor if he could tell him how to get to the famous Windsor-Cornish bridge, the longest covered bridge in New England.

"Yup," replied the old-timer, giving him a hard look, "I could. But I don't know if you'd ever make it."

An old fellow up in Orleans County who had a reputation for being a shrewd man in a deal and tight-fisted to boot, had passed on to his reward, and some of his cronies were talking about the funeral coming up the next day. One suggested that the nicest thing they could do would be to put some folding money in his hand in the coffin. Another agreed to ask his son what he thought of the idea, and if he approved they'd make a collection right away.

The son, evidently a chip off the old block, agreed heartily.

"That's a great idea," he said. "You collect all the bills you can and bring them to me. I'd be glad to write a check for the amount and put it in his hand."

Sometimes we don't count our blessings here. Not so long ago, a Randolph man was visiting his brother who'd moved out to Texas with his family. Both husband and wife were working, so the Randolph man got in the habit of buying his lunch at a small restaurant around the corner. One day, getting up to go, he remarked to the owner that it looked as though they might get a little rain.

"Hope so," said the owner, peering up at the sky. "Not so much for my own sake as for the boy's. I've seen it rain."

When Gil Emmons died—it must have been fifty years ago—he left $20,000 in the savings bank, a goodly sum in those days. Although he left a will some of his heirs were not satisfied and one, who had moved to the city, contested the will and hired "a damn smart city lawyer" to plead his case. The lawyer got friends of the deceased to testify in the hope that he could get one of them to suggest that the deceased was not in his right mind at the time the will was drawn. The first witness, one Bill Cook by name, demonstrated that sometimes even back-country old-timers are a match for sophisticated city lawyers. The interrogation went something like this:

Lawyer: "Did you know Mr. Emmons?"

Cook: "Yes, knew him pretty well."

Lawyer: "Did you see much of him during the last year of his life?"

Cook (cautiously): "Yes, some."

Lawyer: "That's good." Then, pressing his advantage: "This next question is a very important one: When he was alone, did you ever hear Mr. Emmons talking to himself?"

Cook (after thought): "Come to think of it, I never was with Mr. Emmons when he was alone."

A friend of mine has a sightly summer place, up on a hill overlooking Thetford Center. An old-timer had come to do some mowing for him one day and my friend asked if he didn't think the view was nice.

"Yep," said the man, " 'tain't bad at all." Pause. "But it won't buy you no flour."

A fellow who dealt a bit in this and that once stopped at a hill-country farm and said perhaps he'd like to buy a cow. The old farmer allowed as how they were all in the barn and he'd be glad to have him look them over. The dealer picked out a good-looking animal, and after some dickering the price was settled at seventy-five dollars, which he paid. When they got the cow out to put her in the truck, the dealer discovered the animal was stone blind.

"You damn fool," he berated the farmer, "that cow's blind. I can't sell a cow that's blind!"

"Well," said the old-timer, "*I* just did."

Vermonters All

Several years ago there was a very late Spring snow that lured so many skiers to Mount Snow from down-country that the cars were bumper to bumper for more than a mile on the access road. The late Archie Fitzpatrick was in charge of winter work then, and he was plowing the heavy snow with the town truck while his two sons, William and Willard, were standing in the back of the big truck shovelling sand into the spreader as the truck moved slowly along.

Finally the skier right behind him could stand the delay no longer: he pulled out to pass the plow truck, skidded and spun around—having no snow tires—and smashed his pretty grillwork to hell and gone against the side of the truck. Furious, he got out of his car to tongue-lash Archie: "Goddam it, let me see your license!" he shouted.

Archie took a long look at the damage, shook his head and replied: "In Vermont you don't need a license to get run into."

Driving on a back road in Underhill one winter's day, a good Vermonter and a city fellow ran into one another, doing some damage to both cars. The Vermonter walked to a nearby farmhouse and phoned the state police. When he returned, he offered the city man a drink from a bottle he had in his car.

They sat in the car and chatted a while. It took some time for the officer to arrive. The city feller said he was a bit nervous. The Vermonter offered him another drink. After a good swig, the stranger asked if the Vermonter wasn't going to join him.

"Maybe wait until the police have come," the native replied honestly—"and gone."

Some years ago a grizzled farmer, tinkering with a rusty harrow on a back road in Marshfield, was accosted by a bright young man peddling a new manual on soil conservation and improved farm techniques. After explaining how helpful this manual could be, he asked if the farmer would like one. The old man replied:

"Reckon not, son. I don't farm now half as good as I know how to. Got to catch up on what I know before I take on any more ideas."

Not too many years ago, a Vermont farm boy was drafted into the U.S. Army. He was a self-respecting lad in the old tradition, and when he appeared for induction he was neatly dressed with his hair cut and his shoes shined.

The officer in charge was duly impressed, spoke kindly to the boy, and finally asked if there was anything he could do for him to make his stay in the Army a pleasant one.

"Well thank you, there is," said the boy. "When hunting season comes 'round, I'd like some time off so I can go hunting with the boys up on the mountain."

A 1924 clipping from the *Boston Herald* provided this story. The place is the little town of Reading in Windsor County, and the time is the early nineteenth century.

A storekeeper named Levi Grindle had the reputation of being more than a thrifty Vermonter: he was known as a very parsimonious man. Trudging home one day on foot, he was given a lift by one of his neighbors' small boys who was driving a farm cart. On reaching his destination Grindle took out a capacious wallet, fumbled within it, and finally produced a one-penny piece. After some hesitation he gave it to the boy.

The next day the boy, anxious to spend his penny, went into Grindle's store. Seeing a box of figs the boy picked the biggest fig he could find and tendered the penny in payment. Grindle took the fig in one hand and the penny in the other and pondered.

"Quite a lot to give for a penny," he said at last. "Dunno as I can afford it." After due reflection he raised the fig to his mouth, took a generous bite and handed back what was left to the boy, tossing the penny into the till.

"Guess that makes it about right," he said.

A late March snow one year in the Northeast Kingdom prevented the preacher from getting to a funeral in the back-country. The undertaker suggested that in view of this one of the departed's friends and neighbors might like to say a few words.

A long pause ensued. Finally an old-timer stood up and said:

"If no one has anything to say about the deceased brother, I'd like to take a few minutes about the next election."

A man named Bailey was a local captain of industry. In addition to the store he owned water-power privileges and several mills including a sawmill, a small woolen mill, and a gristmill. A neighbor named Hapgood owned several acres of land near Bailey's mills, which, for purposes of expansion, Bailey wished very much to buy. But Hapgood persistently refused to sell and a long-standing feud developed.

Hapgood was the older of the two and in failing health. To make sure that after his death Bailey never got the land he wanted, Hapgood decided to deed the area to the town for a free cemetery, with the proviso that it should never be used for any other purpose.

In due time Hapgood died and was buried in this cemetery. Then folks heard Bailey swear a mighty oath: "By God he can keep me out of the mill-site but bedamned if he can keep me out of the cemetery."

It wasn't until 29 years later that Bailey died, but two stones, only a few yards apart, proved Bailey right and bore silent testimony to the futility of feuds. The inscriptions read:

> DAVID HAPGOOD. DIED 1821, AGED
> 72 YEARS.

> LEVI BAILEY. DIED 1850, AGED 85
> YEARS.

A Burlington couple had given a stained glass window to the church in memory of their dear departed parents, who had worshipped there all their lives.

Desiring a brief story of the window in the local weekly, the lady visited the editor and told him that the major theme in the window was the ascension of Jesus into Heaven as described in the last verses of Luke's Gospel.

"Oh, you should go over and see it," she added. "There is Jesus, attended by angels, going right up to Heaven with Mt. Mansfield in the background."

After forty-one years of public service to his state and the nation, and continuous service in the United States Senate since 1940, George Aiken's announcement in February of 1974 that he would not be a candidate for re-election marked the approaching end of one of the longest and most distinguished careers in Vermont's political history.

Senator Aiken is in so many ways representative of what we call the typical Vermonter that it is not surprising to find that spirit reflected in many of his down-to-earth remarks and comments. He really qualifies as an old-timer.

When asked some years ago if he and Mrs. Aiken were going to Europe that year, his reply was,

"No. Somebody's got to stay home to fill the wood box."

And in a brief letter to former Republican National Committeeman Edward Janeway the Senator explained his decision not to run again for the Senate with one laconic sentence:

"I decided the only way to get a day off was to not run for re-election."

Half these long-standing quarrels we hear about have their origins so far back that most of the time no one, not even their chief participants, remember what they were all about in the first place.

The feud—and that may be a strong word for it—between the Foster and the Chase families in what I've been told was the town of Chelsea was just such an affair as this. Aron Foster wouldn't talk to the Chases. And Bill Chase not only ignored the Fosters but forbade his family to have anything to do with any of them, even the children.

But Mrs. Chase didn't like this state of affairs. She urged her husband to forget and make up. It wasn't Christian to hold a grudge all this time, she kept telling him. She reminded him that the Chases and the Fosters had been close neighbors for years, and she spoke about the old days when the two families had got along fine and had acted as good neighbors should act.

This kind of propaganda went on for quite awhile and ultimately it had its effect. Mrs. Chase realized a thaw was in the making, and she said to her husband one Spring day:

"Bill, you know this'd be a good time to get things back to the way they used to be. Why don't you go right over to the Fosters and ask to borrow their roto-tiller, the one you used to borrow each year? Act like nothing had ever happened; act just like you used to in the old days."

71

Chase thought this over awhile, decided it was a good idea. So he climbed in the pickup and started over to his neighbors.

But before he got there he began thinking. Why should I borrow his old tiller, he asked himself. For heaven's sake, it wasn't as if he didn't have money in the bank to buy one for himself. Maybe Aron wouldn't want to lend it? Why *should* Aron lend it to him anyway, after all those years of silence? Suppose that instead of saying Sure, Foster just gave him a black look and said "Chase, why in hell should I let you have my tiller? What have you done for me recently?" And then I'd look pretty damn silly going back to the wife with an empty truck.

Chase thought some more: I shouldn't take the old tiller even if he pressed it on me, he thought. Probably the best thing would be to give Foster a poke right in the snoot. Why should I be insulted by that fat idiot, just because he has an old tiller he wants to get out of the yard?

At just about this stage in his thinking, Chase arrived at the Foster house. He leaped out of his truck, stomped into the house without knocking, ran into the dining room where he found all the Foster family sitting around the dining room table, looking surprised.

"Foster," he yelled, "I don't want your tiller. You can damn well keep your old tiller. I wouldn't take it if you gave it to me with a sack of turnips. I hope it digs up your best strawberry bed, that's what I hope. You and your damned tiller can go straight to hell."

Then Chase got back in his truck again and drove home, feeling a lot better.

A quotation from the *St. Louis Daily Missouri Republican* of May 27, 1843:

"The people of Vermont are celebrated the world over for morality and uprightness but we were not made aware 'till lately that even their convicted scoundrels were trustworthy.

"The *Mercury* says that a young man recently arrived at Windsor on the stage and applied for admission to the State Prison, showing the papers which entitled him to residence there.

"It seems that he had been convicted in Montpelier of some offense, sentenced to the State Prison for six months and in order to save expense was fitted out with his papers and sent on to Windsor by stage without sheriff or other attendant. On reaching Woodstock the stage by accident left him behind but he coolly waited a day and took the next stage!"

Apropos the recent flood, *The Rutland Herald* published a letter from a former Vermonter who described himself as "transplanted in the desert Southwest," and who recalled the remark of an old farmer during a flood some years earlier:

"I was going to pick some peas for lunch. Now I guess somebody downriver in Connecticut will get them."

Some stories about Calvin Coolidge are true and some are not, and it often becomes difficult to verify the difference. A gentleman in Northampton, Massachusetts, told me this yarn and thinks it is authentic.

You know Mr. and Mrs. Coolidge lived in Northampton most of their adult lives, retired there after their stay in the White House, and Calvin died there.

One morning in that period of retirement, Mr. Coolidge went down to his favorite barbershop for a haircut. The only other customer in the shop at the time was Mr. Coolidge's Northampton physician. Nothing was said between the two men until at one point the doctor turned toward Calvin and asked:

"Mr. President, are you taking the pills I prescribed for you?"

Calvin's terse reply was, "Yes."

The doctor's haircut was finished first. He got on his coat, paid his bill and left the shop. When Calvin got ready to leave, he seemed to be going without paying up. Said the barber, "Mr. Coolidge, I think you are forgetting to pay for your haircut."

"Oh, yes," replied Calvin Coolidge, "I was so busy talking with the doctor I must have forgot."

President Coolidge always tried to spend as much time as possible with his father, Colonel John Coolidge, at the old homestead in Plymouth. During one of these visits his father, who was on the board of directors of the bank in Ludlow, said he should attend a meeting of the board that evening. The President said he would drive him down.

When they arrived some of the directors were visiting outside the bank and Calvin got out of the car with his father and greeted them all. When it came time to go into the meeting, he took his leave with the remark, "Some directors direct: some don't."

President Hoover once remarked to Coolidge that he couldn't understand why his recovery programs had not yet produced results and why his critics were howling so loud.

Coolidge replied, "You can't expect to see calves running the field the day after you put the bull to the cows."

"No," replied Hoover, "But I would expect to see the cows contented."

It was in those dimly but happily remembered days before inflation when old Mrs. Black died "on the town," and the town fathers got Reuben to dig the grave. He dug a nice grave, they planted Mrs. Black, and Reuben put in his bill for ten dollars. The selectmen wouldn't pay it and the question came up in Town Meeting. Reuben put in a powerful plea and wound up with a game-winning clincher:

"By god, I'm going to get ten dollars—or up she comes."

And while we're on the subject of graves, Walter Hard tells the story about the sexton who had managed to hang on to his gravedigger's job for a number of years, but had never been regarded as a model of industry.

A day came when the head of the cemetery association felt a talk was in order.

"Jeb, I don't like to speak of this but it seems to all of us on the committee that each grave you dig is a little shallower than the one before. Can't have that, you know."

"You ain't seen anyone climb out of any of them yet, have you?"

The Old-Timer Will Tell You

That neighbors can be good friends, but it won't pay to be *too* neighborly.

That travel may broaden a man's horizon, but staying home and taking care of the farm puts more in his pocket.

That a dog may be man's best friend, but a good cow is more help at the table.

That Californians like to brag about their weather, but they never have a chance to really appreciate beautiful days the way we do in Vermont—when occasionally we get one.

That while we are told that we can't get along with women but can't get along without them, there often can be middle ground.

That the passing of a good friend, like the felling of a giant pine, leaves a vacant space against the sky.

That "Moonlight and Roses" is a good subject for a song, but sunlight and a good ear of corn does more for the stomach.

That it's nice to sit and think but sometimes it's nicer just to sit.

That what you don't say won't ever hurt you.

That independence is better than riches.

That you can't always judge a cow by her looks.

That if you don't know the difference between east and west, you don't know much.

That silence is golden.

That it's better to wear out than to rust out.

I Want to Thank

these inspired reporters and story-tellers for their generosity: Will Atwood, Roland Boyden, William A. Carter, Sheldon Dimick, Janet Greene, Ralph Nading Hill, Mrs. Neil Malone, Edgar T. Mead, Walter R. Needham, Marguerite Hurrey Wolf. And I'm grateful to my gifted illustrator, John Devaney, for his being so consistently funny: I hope one day to be able to thank him in person.

A. R. F.